What Will You Teach Her?

Michigan Writers Cooperative Press
P. O. Box 2355
Traverse City, Michigan 49685

ISBN-13: 978-1-950744-02-2

Book design by Daniel Stewart

winner
michigan writers cooperative press
2019 poetry contest

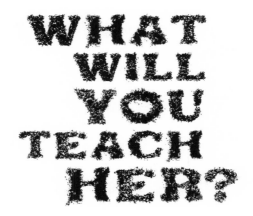

WHAT WILL YOU TEACH HER?

poems by

Megan Klco Kellner

Contents

For my mother, who told me my children would be the key to seeing my world in a new light.

Joy

I called the number on one of those 855-FOR-TRUTH billboards
driving home from a conference in Chicago.
A farmer in Ohio told me women shouldn't work.
You may be happy, he said, but you have no joy.
I had taken the baby with me
walking out of the hotel she saw the sky, itself a bird
alighting over her carseat and startled.
There were drummers cracking 5-gallon buckets on the sidewalk
fast-stepping accompaniment to everyone walking.
I have more joy than I know what to do with.
It swells inside me like those drums snapping louder
the closer we get. I was changing my daughter's diaper
on a bathroom countertop, wiping crust from her eye
I thought how good it is to care for her
how touching her hair is a genuflection.
My son keeps telling me to stop kissing him and I can't.
I push his hair to the side and kiss his head over and over again.
He is the manifestation of all of the love I have for the world
for the trees coughing yellow along the highway, the hokey red billboards
for Christmas Town in Frankenmuth, the purple striations
in the darkening sky that remind me of the padding my mother sewed
into quilts, bleached grass yellow
a backdrop to my whole life in Michigan, anemic along the roadside
and in the field behind our neighborhood before they peppered it
with prefab houses. We used to gather winter bouquets out there
collected seed heads and shoved them into a vase in the living room
where the nodding hydrangeas slowly shed tan petals.
He told me I have no joy
that when something bad happens
I will lose my happiness.

Happiness is a seed
locked in a dried up flower head waiting for light.
To have eyes like my daughter's
like cups, peering out from the small hole in her carseat cover
open as if drinking the confetti of leaves and chattering families
walking with strollers and buses and trampled flyers screaming at the dirt,

to have joy is to be awake to the drumming drumming drumming
from the man at the bucket
as if his happiness shakes his bones, forces his arms up and down
bursts out like a shoot from within him.

Morning

Oh here it is

the quiet morning
before my husband and son wake up
after I've gotten my fix of news and coffee that both
wind a string inside me
before I run a finger on my son's forearm
to gently tell him that it is time to get ready for school
before he whimpers, 'No mommy.'

It is hard to be alive
hard to be present in this quiet morning
when there is only yourself
and the refrigerator-like hum
of your own blood in your ears
the soft ruffling of your child turning over
on the baby monitor.

I try to avoid it each morning
with a news app on my phone
and my Facebook thread.

I haven't mastered my father's art of slowly making coffee
patiently waiting by the french press
and staring out the window.

My mother, a knife,
cuts through the morning
clattering dishes and fixing breakfast for everyone
even if they do not live with her.

I watched her baking once
hypnotized
by the way she stirred buttermilk
letting it kiss the lip of the bowl
without spilling over.

She and her mind and her hand
were all in that quiet morning together
filling it with light
controlling the slow pull of the sun
into the world.

To be present is to raise the morning.
To swallow grilled ham on bread
is to take communion
in the daily resurrection of the world.

Maybe the news on my phone will be different
or maybe I'll be better able to bear it
with sunlight inside me
a glimpse at a woodpecker in the yard
and a quiet look at my hands
on our scratched kitchen table.

She is the Cup

My daughter chuckled when I kissed her face this morning
the deep, throaty laugh
of an older woman

Her face is a light
firefly bursting in the treeline

Sometimes when we nurse she unlatches and smiles
and milk flows into my clothing
where it sours

The white pine in the backyard will hollow out from the inside
this house will fall

She is the cup into which I pour my daily gratitude

She is light continuing

My Family, Sick on a Sunday

There's a window in the shower
that looks out on the backyard so in the morning
I watch steam soften the pine trees
into dark shapes. It's Sunday
and both the kids are sick.
I called three doctor's offices
to see if I have to take Clara to the ER
for a fever over 102.
Taking a shower is a holy act.
In Morocco, traveling with a friend
we couldn't afford a hostel with a bath so
our first day back we scrubbed our bodies
of eight days of dust and tannery smells
and our skin rolled up into little brown pills
that peppered our towels.
Justin was out duck hunting this morning.
He comes from the Upper Peninsula
where his feet never warm
and snakes crawl into the walls at camp
to get out of the cold.
Our whole world now is four small rooms.
Charles beats a path into the carpet with his slippered feet,
Clara screams when she leaves my body,
we stitch closer to one another
on the old plaid sofa and watch the same movies
over and over, stroking their hair.
It's our fault for taking them trick-or-treating in the rain
yesterday, running from stop to stop
between SUVs parked in a semicircle
in a gray church parking lot. We are so impatient
to show them the world
that we carried them out in the mist
pointing to all the kids in their soggy costumes,
bouncing them on our hips,
singing.

Not a Good Mother

Fake white lilies in the
Goodyear lobby stink
—dust and rubber.
Who has time to care for flowers
between back-to-back tire rotations?
We bought a goldfish two weeks ago.
My son carried it home carefully
in its plastic bag. It's dead already
floated in cloudy, yellow water
in an old flower vase.
There is no time to feed ourselves.
Speaking at a meeting, I felt the hot sting
of milk rushing into my breasts
slowly wetting my shirt
revealing my other body
soft as a baked apple.
I wanted to make the strudel my mother
used to make in fall
that wasn't hers but belonged to
three generations of flour-caked hands on rolling pins.
She used to pack baloney sandwiches back into the bread bags
and freeze them when we were young.
I should have known better than to have entrusted another life to myself.
My fingers fumble
unbuckling the baby from her carseat after work.
It feels slothful to wait on this vinyl sofa
for a flat tire patch
with these plastic lilies pretending to be gracious.
I'm fantasizing about slicing apples
while my son colors at the kitchen table.
Maybe we have Halloween songs on the stereo,
maybe I deliver strudel wrapped in tin foil to the woman next door.
I sat in the backyard drinking wine with her once.
She wiped lipstick from her glass and said flatly,
"I wasn't a good mother,"
the way I'd say I quit piano lessons
that I don't know how to change a tire.

MEGAN KLCO KELLNER

The Baby Still Sleeps On My Chest

In the afternoon we are one
wave, rising and falling together.
She hunts for my nipple like she's
digging in earth, like she's
nosing my chest into the shape
of the basket beds the deer tuck
their bodies into. Their mothers' chests
must be horizons, too. When I walk out of the room,
she screams.
Earth flings open.
Sky unwinds.

Our House

The neighbors have been here 50 years.
They used to rent a converted chicken coop
behind our house, the farmhouse.
The only evidence is the split concrete pad in the backyard
the occasional scrap of metal kicked up
by the lawnmower.

In our last house the basement walls
used to crumble and weep when it rained.
It's strange to me my kids won't remember
the stale smell of mildew growing behind plaster
to them it will just be stories.

I am trying to remember my life before them
before my son was born. I was working in a gunshop
carving checkers into rifle stocks, came home one day
panicked and dizzy thinking
chemicals had soaked under my gloves.

I kept picturing a shadow on the ultrasound
where the heart should be.

Our house has a memory of five families,
we're told.
I've been searching for them in the layers of laminate floor
above the drop ceiling in the kitchen
in the hole punched into the inside of a closet door.
My husband keeps finding toys lost out in the woods
Hot Wheels and Lego figures
a dried-out bouncy ball cracked like surface of Mars.

Our signature is the dirt that's gathering
inside the windowsills
in the grout in the shower.

When I lived alone I let the dishes pile up in the sink.
Now I bend every two steps to pick up a sock
or a tossed diaper, a reverse sower
gathering spent seeds.

Wind

Your inner world is expanding,
new planets formed by dust and gravity.
Every word I say to you
swirls somewhere inside you
echoes back to me.

Sometimes your body can't hold the wind
pushing out from within your limbs.

You thrash on the kitchen floor.

Thirst

When you were born your dad asked me,
"What will you teach her?"

That summer we found twenty-six cicada shells
sliced
clinging to tree trunks in the backyard.

You were softer than my own split body,
iridescent.

You are becoming straighter.
You push down against my legs when I hold you
and lunge toward the glass sliding door.

Outside red-breasted nuthatches hop along the deck rail.
The mulberry is swirling
on fire with evening light and dancing warblers diving
for insects.

You have the face of someone who's been trapped underground.
You reach in jerking motions
forward
forward.

At night you burrow your head into my body
dig your fingernails into my breast
thrash your head from side to side and yank my nipple.

Your world is alive
with dancing color patches
flashing like leaves trembling
and hunger
the desperate need to be filled
as if your body were a sieve through which all sensation passes,
the warmth of my fingers on your neck
the cold draft from the sliding door

the sudden joy when you see a face
or hear a familiar voice.

What can I teach you that you do not know already?
You like to be held upright
eyes darting side to side
hands clenching and unclenching
milking the air.

I want to teach you to thirst the way hummingbirds do.
I have a red hat I can't wear in the backyard because
they dive for it.

Handprint

I still can't believe you are real

You left a sticky handprint on the bathroom sink
I don't want to scrub off because it's somehow a record
of your wild sweetness

You will grow into someone I will not recognize

Espaliered boy,
stretched wide and tall to make a man

Stay

stay, stay, my son begs
at drop off
at bedtime, his voice
made small
like the whinging we heard from inside the owl box
my husband unstuffed with leaves this spring.
He stuck his phone through the opening
and caught a picture of a blue back,
serif tail curled under. Blue as galaxy
as ocean trench, as blood.
There was no chattering, though,
no frantic pleading from the trees nearby
no whimpering when he closed the lid just
shuffling, leaves against each other.
I want to make something like a nest
of things I've fished from my daughter's mouth:
acorn cap, hairtie, googly eye
from the snot smeared on my shoulder
while she's tucked into my hip.
I read about this artist
who dug litter from the Thames
and arranged it on white pedestals. Somebody's bit
of shoe sole rubber gravely considered
at the Tate. There is no art
to the losing of things
to the lonely blue creature in the owl box,
the drifting needles of the Norway pine
that fungus is nibbling to a fishbone,
the lost toys my son wept over
or the bruises that puddle
and evaporate along his shin bones
like so much summer rain.
I cannot save the shell of his body that clings to me.
There was a woman
in our driveway once with a mouth
so choked with old words that her son, a man,
spoke for her: *Is there still*

a boulder split in two in the backyard?
and I think I was in a hurry, so
I tried to be polite which means
I didn't get to ask them how it broke.

First World

Ancient pain cleaved you from me
a splitting of bones no one feels
anymore at least not in this neighborhood with its matching
pastel bungalows

A dark first world that terrifies you now
so you sleep with a flashlight in your bed
that crowns you
an aurora borealis on the baby monitor

I still feel phantom kicks in my stomach
when my body misses you

You were me
once

Do you miss it?

Working

It snowed today.

I need to wrap my hands around a cup.
The handmade one with a thumbprint
where the potter squeezed it when she
pried it off the wheel.
I rest my finger in the dimple where hers was
drinking coffee at the table.

The potted plant on the deck is still
blooming fuchsia, dressed in ice
still celebrating a summer birth.
I'll probably forget it out on the deck rail all winter.

All my hands do is dress and undress my children.

Who am I when I'm not working?
The dented pot out in the sandbox
is a swimming pool, a hat.
I am a weaver passing a shuttle back and forth
stacking days on each other.

What If She is a Lost Monument

I spent the evening on my knees, clapping
my hands in front of the baby's face while the smoke
from some building on the news turned white
noise on all channels.
The idea that she is lost, is a place I cannot visit
is as violent as fire.
When I say her name
she keeps on digging her fingers into the shag
for some lost crumb and I'm picturing
stained glass shattering, kaleidoscope pains
wonders countless as the shining insects
scrabbling the Amazon where that grand museum
burned to dust
whole languages lost in its crypts and computers
– all sealed in her soft body,
a sacred host.
I wanted to grab her wrists, force
her palms together to give rhythm to her joy
at seeing my sunlight. Maybe
if I weave enough words through her ears
she will open at the binding,
she will answer to the name we gave her,
she will mirror, if not my motions, then the shape
of my sadness at not getting to know her
more completely.

Lived In

The windy parking lot at my son's daycare
is as cleansing as my daily shower.
I'm embarrassed
by the peeling topcoat on the side of my Pontiac Vibe.
The floor in the backseat is an offering of plastic toys mixed with
crushed leaves and Alka-Seltzer from a would-be science project.
Another mom remarked that it was
lived in.

Lived in
like my son's shoes with sand shoved up under the lining
lived in like the plaid pull-out sofa that still holds my shape
from where I nursed my two children.

This weekend we were watching my son play on the kitchen floor
and I felt the same comfort I used to feel
lying on my grandpa's sofa
falling asleep to the golf channel under a brown and yellow afghan.

I wonder what he'll remember of this time.
Mornings tugging his fingers into the right holes in his gloves
it's so easy for me to lose patience.

Today he clung to me at drop off
begging.

He and I are slowly separating
the way branches grow apart at angles.
I wonder if my mother ever lost the desperate urge
to kiss her children.

I keep thinking of those words
lived in
like a knotted burl
my own soft stomach
my crooked arms.

Alive on Knapp ST

Trees screaming color.
My blood made their sound when you were born.
On the radio, people chanting in Hebrew
for the victims of the synagogue shooting.
There must be screams rising in their throats
hot as swallowed coals.
Clara went to the ER last night
fever burning through her body
straightened each of her fingers, forcing
her hands open.
My neck stiffens when I listen to the news
spread the lie that people are enemies to one another.
I have to keep lifting my head
above the steering wheel
to watch the rows of trees pass
exhaling yellow honey smell.
Driving
everything starts to compress
water tower graffiti
the color of school busses
red and blue balloons at the car dealership
odd bits of painted signs still showing up in building corners.
The way everything is burning at the edges
blades of long grass turning gradually yellow then brown
withering as if dipped in iodine
faint drifting smell of hay.
Fever is burning through my baby,
life fighting microscopic life.
Her body is learning that it is discreet.
Public radio switches to Wagner after the news
and a slow crescendo of violins builds in my body
a deep, long breath.
I've started to catalogue what is unkeepable.
The changing trees, the mourners in the temple chanting
the shattering cry I passed on to you at birth
trees catching fire in November
all rage at dying.
I am angry that things will happen without me.

MICHIGAN WRITERS COOPERATIVE PRESS would like to express our thanks to Casey Thayer for judging the poetry manuscripts in our chapbook contest this year, and for editing Megan's winning chapbook. We are grateful for his commitment of time, energy, and expertise to all of the contestants' manuscripts. Thank you, Casey, for helping Michigan Writers Cooperative Press develop and publish this new poetic voice.

About the Judge

CASEY THAYER is the author of the full-length poetry collection, *Self Portrait with Spurs and Sulfur* (University of New Mexico Press, 2015). Casey holds an MFA in poetry from Northern Michigan University. He was a Wallace Stegner fellow at Stanford University and has been a fellow at the Sewanee Writers' Conference. His work is widely published in journals and magazines, including *American Poetry Review, North American Review,* and *Poetry*. Currently, he lives in Chicago and works at the University of Illinois at Chicago.

About the Author

MEGAN KLCO KELLNER is an award-winning visual artist who began writing poems in earnest during late-night feedings after her children were born. She holds an MFA in Painting from Kendall College of Art & Design and teaches children and adults to be visual explorers through art- and science-based education programs at Frederik Meijer Gardens & Sculpture Park. She and her husband are planting flowers, watching birds and trying to raise two good humans in Grand Rapids, Michigan. You can follow her work at www.meganklco.com.

About Michigan Writers Cooperative Press

This book was published in the spring of 2019 in a signed edition of 100 copies.

This chapbook is part of the Cooperative Series of the Michigan Writers Small Press Project, which was launched in 2005 to give members of Michigan Writers, Inc. a new avenue to publication. All of the chapbooks in this series are an author's first book in that genre. The Coop Press shoulders the publishing costs for the first edition, and writers share the marketing and promotional responsibilities in return for the prestige of being published by a press that prints only carefully selected manuscripts.

Chapbook length manuscripts of poetry, short stories, and essays are solicited each year from members and adjudicated by a panel of experienced writers and a judge who is a specialist in a particular genre. For more information, please visit www.michwriters.org.

MICHIGAN WRITERS is an open-membership organization dedicated to providing opportunities for networking, professional growth, and publication for writers of all ages and skill levels in Northwest Michigan and beyond.

MANAGING EDITOR: Kevin Avery

CONTEST READERS: Robb Astor, Anthony Guerriero, Jennifer Kirkpatrick Johnson, Susan Odgers, John Pahl, Karen Stein, Daniel Stewart, Patricia Trentacoste, Sarah Wangler

BOOK DESIGN: Daniel Stewart

Other Titles Available
from Michigan Writers Cooperative Press

Michigan WRITERS

Made in the USA
Columbia, SC
26 May 2019